DATE			
APR 17 2006			

DISCARDED

The Quiet Hour

Henry Howard, Earl of Surrey

From the drawing by Hans Holbein

(The name in the upper left is incorrect, and was added
by a later hand)

The Quiet Hour

Selected and arranged by
FitzRoy Carrington

*" Happy those early days, when I
Shined in my angel-infancy ! "*
Henry Vaughan.

Granger Index Reprint Series

BOOKS FOR LIBRARIES PRESS
FREEPORT, NEW YORK

First Published 1915
Reprinted 1971

INTERNATIONAL STANDARD BOOK NUMBER:
0-8369-6264-8

LIBRARY OF CONGRESS CATALOG CARD NUMBER:
71-160901

PRINTED IN THE UNITED STATES OF AMERICA

To
My Wife

Years pass, hopes fade, ambitions change their
    course;
Love changes not, is old yet ever new.
Since *The Queen's Garland* first I twined for you
Full eighteen years have spent their shaping force.
Together *The Kings' Lyrics* we have heard,
The Pilgrim's Staff guiding our wearied feet,
The Shepherd's Pipe to us has sounded sweet,
And sweet has seemed each rustic, answering word.

Together still, we share *The Quiet Hour*
With boys and girls, who make the "quiet" seem
Some far, faint echo of an enchanted dream
Magicians weave by necromantic power!
Sweetheart, Wife, Mother; loving, tender, true,
This little book I dedicate to you.

FitzRoy Carrington

June 7, 1915

Contents

Cradle Songs

Infancy

Childhood

Night

Sleep

Charms

Dirges

Illustrations

Part I
Cradle Songs

The Quiet Hour

How the Age of Children is the Happiest if they had Skill to understand it

LAID in my quiet bed, in study as I were,
I saw within my troubled head a heap of thoughts
appear.
And every thought did show so lively in mine eyes,
That now I sigh'd, and then I smil'd, as cause of
thought did rise.
I saw the little boy in thought how oft that he
Did wish of God to scape the rod, a tall young
man to be.
The young man eke that feels his bones with
pains opprest,
How he would be a rich old man, to live and die
at rest.
The rich old man that sees his end draw on so
sore,
How he would be a boy again, to live so much the
more.

Whereat full oft I smiled, to see how all these
    three,
From boy to man, from man to boy, would chop
    and change degree.

  .   .   .   .

Whereat I sigh'd and said: 'Farewell! my wonted
    joy;
Truss up thy pack, and trudge from me to every
    little boy;
And tell them thus from me; their time most
    happy is,
If, to their time, they reason had, to know the
    truth of this.'

Henry Howard, Earl of Surrey.

Balow

Balow, my babe, lie still and sleep!
It grieves me sore to see thee weep.
Wouldst thou lie quiet I'se be glad,
Thy mourning makes my sorrow sad:
Balow my boy, thy mother's joy,
Thy father breeds me great annoy —
    Balow, la-low!

When he began to court my love,
And with his sugred words me move,

His faynings false and flattering cheer
To me that time did not appear:
But now I see most cruellye
He care ne for my babe nor me —
    Balow, la-low!

Lie still, my darling, sleep awhile,
And when thou wak'st thou 'le sweetly smile:
But smile not as thy father did,
To cozen maids: nay, God forbid!
But yet I fear thou wilt go near
Thy father's heart and face to bear —
    Balow, la-low!

I cannot choose but ever will|
Be loving to thy father still;
Where'er he go, where'er he ride,
My love with him doth still abide;
In weal or woe, where'er he go,
My heart shall ne'er depart him fro —
    Balow, la-low!

But do not, do not, pretty mine,
To faynings false thy heart incline!
Be loyal to thy lover true,
And never change her for a new:

If good or fair, of her have care,
For woman's banning's wondrous sare —
      Balow, la-low!

Bairn, by thy face I will beware;
Like Siren's words, I'll come not near;
My babe and I together will live;
He'll comfort me when cares do grieve.
My babe and I right soft will lie,
And ne'er respect man's crueltye —
      Balow, la-low!

Farewell, farewell, the falsest youth
That ever kist a woman's mouth!
I wish all maids be warn'd by me
Never to trust man's courtesye;
For if we do but chance to bow,
They'll use us then they care not how —
      Balow, la-low!

                  Anonymous, Sixteenth Century.

A Sweet Lullaby

COME little babe, come silly soul,
Thy father's shame, thy mother's grief,
Born as I doubt to all our dole,
And to thyself unhappy chief:

Sing lullaby and lap it warm,
Poor soul that thinks no creature harm.

Thou little think'st and less dost know,
The cause of this thy mother's moan;
Thou want'st the wit to wail her woe,
And I myself am all alone:
 Why dost thou weep? why dost thou wail?
 And know'st not yet what thou dost ail.

Come little wretch, ah, silly heart,
Mine only joy, what can I more?
If there be any wrong thy smart,
That may the destinies implore:
 'T was I, I say, against my will,
 I wail the time, but be thou still.

And dost thou smile? Oh thy sweet face,
Would God Himself He might thee see,
No doubt thou would'st soon purchase grace,
I know right well, for thee and me:
 But come to mother, babe, and play,
 For father false is fled away.

Sweet boy, if it by fortune chance
Thy father home again to send,

If death do strike me with his lance,
Yet mayst thou me to him commend:
    If any ask thy mother's name,
    Tell how by love she purchased blame.

Then will his gentle heart soon yield:
I know him of a noble mind:
Although a lion in the field,
A lamb in town thou shalt him find:
    Ask blessing, babe, be not afraid,
    His sugar'd words hath me betrayed.

Then mayst thou joy and be right glad;
Although in woe I seem to moan,
Thy father is no rascal lad,
A noble youth of blood and bone:
    His glancing looks, if he once smile,
    Right honest women may beguile.

Come little boy and rock a-sleep,
Sing lullaby and be thou still;
I that can do naught else but weep,,
Will sit by thee and wail my fill:
    God bless my babe, and lullaby,
    From this thy father's quality.

Nicholas Breton.

Sephestia's Lullaby

WEEP not, my wanton, smile upon my knee;
When thou art old there's grief enough for thee.
    Mother's wag, pretty boy,
    Father's sorrow, father's joy;
    When thy father first did see
    Such a boy by him and me,
    He was glad, I was woe;
    Fortune changèd made him so,
    When he left his pretty boy,
    Last his sorrow, first his joy.

Weep not, my wanton, smile upon my knee;
When thou art old there's grief enough for thee.
    Streaming tears that never stint,
    Like pearl-drops from a flint,
    Fell by course from his eyes,
    That one another's place supplies;
    Thus he grieved in every part,
    Tears of blood fell from his heart,
    When he left his pretty boy,
    Father's sorrow, father's joy..

Weep not, my wanton, smile upon my knee;
When thou art old there's grief enough for thee.

The wanton smiled, father wept,
Mother cried, baby leapt;
More he crow'd, more we cried,
Nature could not sorrow hide:
He must go, he must kiss
Child and mother, baby-bliss,
For he left his pretty boy,
Father's sorrow, father's joy.
Weep not, my wanton, smile upon my knee;
When thou art old there's grief enough for thee.

Robert Greene.

Lullaby

Upon my lap my sovereign sits
And sucks upon my breast;
Meantime his love maintains my life
And gives my sense her rest.
    Sing lullaby, my little boy,
    Sing lullaby, mine only joy!

When thou hast taken thy repast,
Repose, my babe, on me;
So may thy mother and thy nurse
Thy cradle also be.
    Sing lullaby, my little boy,
    Sing lullaby, mine only joy!

I grieve that duty doth not work
All that my wishing would;
Because I would not be to thee
But in the best I should.
    Sing lullaby, my little boy,
    Sing lullaby, mine only joy!

Yet as I am, and as I may,
I must and will be thine,
Though all too little for thyself
Vouchsafing to be mine.
    Sing lullaby, my little boy,
    Sing lullaby, mine only joy!

Richard Rowlands.

Lullaby

GOLDEN slumbers kiss your eyes,
Smiles awake you when you rise.
Sleep, pretty wantons, do not cry,
And I will sing a lullaby:
Rock them, rock them, lullaby.

Care is heavy, therefore sleep you;
You are care, and care must keep you.
Sleep, pretty wantons, do not cry,
And I will sing a lullaby:
Rock them, rock them, lullaby.

Thomas Dekker.

A Cradle Hymn

Hush! my dear, lie still and slumber,
  Holy Angels guard thy bed!
Heavenly blessings without number
  Gently falling on thy head.

Sleep, my babe; thy food and raiment,
  House and home, thy friends provide;
All without thy care or payment,
  All thy wants are well supplied.

How much better thou'rt attended
  Than the Son of God could be,
When from heaven He descended,
  And became a child like thee!

Soft and easy is thy cradle:
  Coarse and hard thy Saviour lay,
When His birthplace was a stable
  And His softest bed was hay.

　　·　　·　　·　　·　　·　　·

See the kinder shepherds round Him,
  Telling wonders from the sky!
Where they sought Him, there they found Him,
  With His Virgin-Mother by.

See the lovely babe a-dressing;
    Lovely infant, how He smiled!
When He wept, the mother's blessing
    Soothed and hush'd the holy child.

Lo, He slumbers in His manger,
    Where the hornèd oxen fed;
Peace, my darling, here's no danger;
    Here's no ox anear thy bed.

May'st thou live to know and fear Him,
    Trust and love Him all thy days;
Then go dwell for ever near Him,
    See His face, and sing His praise!

Isaac Watts.

A Cradle Song

Sleep, sleep, beauty bright,
Dreaming in the joys of night;
Sleep, sleep, in thy sleep
Little sorrows sit and weep.

Sweet babe, in thy face
Soft desires I can trace,
Secret joys and secret smiles,
Little pretty infant wiles.

As thy softest limbs I feel,
Smiles as of the morning steal
O'er thy cheek, and o'er thy breast
Where thy little heart doth rest.

O the cunning wiles that creep
In thy little heart asleep!
When thy little heart doth wake,
Then the dreadful light shall break.

William Blake.

The Land of Dreams

AWAKE, awake, my little boy!
Thou wast thy mother's only joy.
Why dost thou weep in thy gentle sleep?
Awake! thy father doth thee keep.

'O, what land is the Land of Dreams?
What are its mountains and what are its streams?'
'O father! I saw my mother there,
Among the lilies by waters fair.'

'Among the lambs, clothèd in white,
She walk'd with her Thomas in sweet delight.
I wept for joy, like a dove I mourn —
O when shall I again return?'

William Blake

From the painting by Thomas Phillips

'Dear child! I also by pleasant streams
Have wandered all night in the Land of Dreams;
But though calm and warm the waters wide,
I could not get to the other side.'

'Father, O father! what do we here?
In this land of unbelief and fear?
The Land of Dreams is better far,
Above the light of the morning star.'

William Blake.

Lullaby

THE rook's nest do rock on the tree-top
Where vew foes can stand;
The martin's is high, an' is deep
In the steep cliff o' zand.
But thou, love, a-sleepin' where vootsteps
Mid come to thy bed,
Hast father an' mother to watch thee
An' shelter thy head.
    Lullaby, Lilybrow. Lie asleep;
    Blest be thy rest.

An' zome birds do keep under ruffèn
Their young vrom the storm,
An' zome wi' nest-hoodens o' moss
An' o' wool, do lie warm.

An' we wull look well to the house ruf
That o'er thee mid leäk,
An' the blast that mid beät on thy winder
Shall not smite thy cheäk.
Lullaby, Lilybrow. Lie asleep;
Blest be thy rest.

William Barnes.

O Sleep, My Babe

O SLEEP, my babe, hear not the rippling wave,
Nor feel the breeze that round thee ling'ring
strays
To drink thy balmy breath,
And sigh one long farewell.

Soon shall it mourn above thy wat'ry bed,
And whisper to me, on the wave-beat shore,
Deep murm'ring in reproach,
Thy sad untimely fate.

Ere those dear eyes had open'd on the light,
In vain to plead, thy coming life was sold,
O waken'd but to sleep,
Whence it can wake no more!

A thousand and a thousand silken leaves
The tufted beech unfolds in early spring,
    All clad in tenderest green,
    All of the selfsame shape:

A thousand infant faces, soft and sweet,
Each year sends forth, yet every mother views
    Her last not least beloved
    Like its dear self alone.

No musing mind hath ever yet foreshaped
The face to-morrow's sun shall first reveal,
    No heart hath e'er conceived
    What love that face will bring.

O sleep, my babe, nor heed how mourns the gale
To part with thy soft locks and fragrant breath,
    As when it deeply sighs
    O'er autumn's latest bloom.
                      Sara Coleridge.

A Christmas Lullaby

SLEEP, baby, sleep! the Mother sings:
Heaven's angels kneel and fold their wings.
    Sleep, baby, sleep!

With swathes of scented hay Thy bed
By Mary's hand at eve was spread.
      Sleep, baby, sleep!

At midnight came the shepherds, they
Whom seraphs wakened by the way.
      Sleep, baby, sleep!

And three kings from the East afar
Ere dawn came guided by Thy star.
      Sleep, baby, sleep!

They brought Thee gifts of gold and gems,
Pure orient pearls, rich diadems.
      Sleep, baby, sleep!

But Thou who liest slumbering there,
Art King of Kings, earth, ocean, air.
      Sleep, baby, sleep!

Sleep, baby, sleep! the shepherds sing:
Through heaven, through earth, hosannas ring.
      Sleep, baby, sleep.

John Addington Symonds.

Part II
Infancy

The Retreat

HAPPY those early days, when I
Shined in my Angel-infancy!
Before I understood this place
Appointed for my second race,
Or taught my soul to fancy ought
But a white celestial thought:
When yet I had not walk'd above
A mile or two from my first Love.
And looking back — at that short space —
Could see a glimpse of His bright face:
When on some gilded cloud, or flow'r,
My gazing soul would dwell an hour,
And in those weaker glories spy
Some shadows of eternity:
Before I taught my tongue to wound
My Conscience with a sinful sound,
Or had the black art to dispense
A several sin to ev'ry sense,
But felt through all this fleshly dress
Bright shoots of everlastingness.

O how I long to travel back,
And tread again that ancient track!

That I might once more reach that plain
Where first I left my glorious train;
From whence th' enlighten'd spirit sees
That shady City of palm-trees.
But ah! my soul with too much stay
Is drunk, and staggers in the way!
Some men a forward motion love,
But I by backward steps would move;
And when this dust falls to the urn,
In that state I came, return.

Henry Vaughan.

The Salutation

THESE little limbs,
These eyes and hands which here I find,
These rosy cheeks wherewith my life begins,
Where have ye been? behind
What curtain were ye from me hid so long,
Where was, in that abyss, my speaking tongue?

When silent I
So many thousand, thousand years
Beneath the dust did in a chaos lie,
How could I smiles or tears,
Or lips or hands or eyes or ears perceive?
Welcome ye treasures which I now receive.

I that so long
　Was nothing from eternity,
Did little think such joys as ear or tongue
　To celebrate or see:
Such sounds to hear, such hands to feel, such feet,
Beneath the skies on such a ground to meet.

　New burnisht joys!
　Which yellow gold and pearls excel!
Such sacred treasures are the limbs in boys,
　In which a soul doth dwell;
Their organized joints and azure veins
More wealth include than all the world contains.

　From dust I rise,
　And out of nothing now awake,
Then brighter regions which salute mine eyes,
　A gift from God I take.
The earth, the seas, the light, the day, the skies,
The sun and stars are mine; if those I prize.

　Long time before
　I in my mother's womb was born,
A God preparing did this glorious store,
　The world for me adorn.
Into this Eden so divine and fair,
So wide and bright, I come His son and heir.

A stranger here
Strange things doth meet, strange glories see;
Strange treasures lodg'd in this fair world appear,
Strange all and new to me;
But that they mine should be, who nothing was,
That strangest is of all, yet brought to pass.

Thomas Traherne.

Innocence

BUT that which most I wonder at, which most
I did esteem my bliss, which most I boast,
And ever shall enjoy, is that within
I felt no stain nor spot of sin.

No darkness then did overshade,
But all within was pure and bright,
No guilt did crush nor fear invade,
But all my soul was full of light.

A joyful sense and purity
Is all I can remember,
The very night to me was bright,
'Twas Summer in December.

Thomas Traherne.

The Rapture

SWEET infancy!
O fire of heaven! O sacred light!
How fair and bright!
How great am I,
Whom all the world doth magnify!

O heavenly joy!
O great and sacred blessedness
Which I possess!
So great a joy
Who did into our arms convey!

From God above
Being sent, the Heavens me enflame:
To praise His name
The stars do move!
The burning sun doth shew His love.

O how divine
Am I! To all this sacred wealth,
This life and health,
Who raised? Who mine
Did make the same? What hand divine?

Thomas Traherne.

The Lamb

LITTLE lamb, who made thee?
Dost thou know who made thee?
Gave thee life and bid thee feed,
By the stream and o'er the mead;
Gave thee clothing of delight,
Softest clothing, wooly, bright,
Gave thee such a tender voice,
Making all the vales rejoice?
 Little lamb, who made thee?
 Dost thou know who made thee?

 Little lamb, I 'll tell thee,
 Little lamb, I 'll tell thee:
He is callèd by thy name,
For He calls Himself a lamb.
He is meek, and He is mild;
He became a little child.
I a child, and thou a lamb,
We are callèd by His name.
 Little lamb, God bless thee!
 Little lamb, God bless thee!

William Blake.

Infant Joy

"I HAVE no name:
 I am but two days old."
 What shall I call thee?
"I happy am,
 Joy is my name."
 Sweet joy befall thee!

 Pretty joy!
 Sweet joy, but two days old.
 Sweet joy I call thee:
 Thou dost smile,
 I sing the while,
 Sweet joy befall thee!

William Blake.

Infant Sorrow

My mother groan'd, my father wept;
Into the dangerous world I leapt,
Helpless, naked, piping loud,
Like a fiend hid in a cloud.

Struggling in my father's hands,
Striving against my swaddling-bands,
Bound and weary, I thought best
To sulk upon my mother's breast.

William Blake.

Nurse's Song

WHEN the voices of children are heard on the
    green,
  And laughing is heard on the hill,
My heart is at rest within my breast,
  And everything else is still.

"Then come home, my children, the sun is gone
    down,
  And the dews of night arise;
Come, come, leave off play, and let us away
  Till the morning appears in the skies."

"No, no, let us play, for it is yet day,
  And we cannot go to sleep;
Besides, in the sky the little birds fly,
  And the hills are all cover'd with sheep."

"Well, well, go and play till the light fades away,
  And then go home to bed."
The little ones leapèd and shoutèd and laugh'd
  And all the hills echoèd.

William Blake.

Ode
Intimations of Immortality
from Recollections of
Early Childhood

THERE was a time when meadow, grove, and
    stream,
The earth, and every common sight,
      To me did seem
    Apparell'd in celestial light,
The glory and the freshness of a dream.
It is not now as it hath been of yore; —
    Turn wheresoe'er I may,
    By night or day,
The things which I have seen I now can see no
    more.

    The rainbow comes and goes,
    And lovely is the rose;
    The moon doth with delight
Look round her when the heavens are bare;
    Waters on a starry night
    Are beautiful and fair;
    The sunshine is a glorious birth;
    But yet I know, where'er I go,
That there hath pass'd away a glory from the earth.

Now, while the birds thus sing a joyous song,
  And while the young lambs bound
   As to the tabor's sound,
To me alone there came a thought of grief:
A timely utterance gave that thought relief,
  And I again am strong:
The cataracts blow their trumpets from the
  steep;
No more shall grief of mine the season wrong;
I hear the echoes through the mountains throng,
The winds come to me from the fields of sleep,
  And all the earth is gay;
   Land and sea
  Give themselves up to jollity,
   And with the heart of May
  Doth every heart keep holiday; —
   Thou Child of Joy,
Shout round me, let me hear thy shouts, thou
  happy Shepherd-boy!

Ye blessèd creatures, I have heard the call
  Ye to each other make; I see
The heavens laugh with you in your jubilee;
  My heart is at your festival,
   My head hath its coronal,
The fulness of your bliss, I feel — I feel it all.

William Wordsworth

From the painting by H. W. Pickersgill

O evil day! if I were sullen
While the Earth herself is adorning
   This sweet May-morning,
And the children are pulling
   On every side,
In a thousand valleys far and wide,
Fresh flowers; while the sun shines warm,
And the babe leaps up on his mother's arm: —
   I hear, I hear, with joy I hear!
   — But there's a tree, of many, one,
A single field which I have look'd upon,
Both of them speak of something that is gone;
   The pansy at my feet
   Doth the same tale repeat:
   Whither is fled the visionary gleam?
   Where is it now, the glory and the dream?

Our birth is but a sleep and a forgetting:
The Soul that rises with us, our life's Star,
   Hath had elsewhere its setting,
   And cometh from afar:
   Not in entire forgetfulness,
   And not in utter nakedness,
But trailing clouds of glory do we come
   From God, who is our home:
Heaven lies about us in our infancy!

Shades of the prison-house begin to close
    Upon the growing Boy,
But he beholds the light, and whence it flows
    He sees it in his joy;
The Youth, who daily farther from the east
    Must travel, still is Nature's priest,
    And by the vision splendid
    Is on his way attended;
At length the Man perceives it die away,
And fade into the light of common day.

Earth fills her lap with pleasures of her own;
Yearnings she hath in her own natural kind,
And, even with something of a mother's mind,
    And no unworthy aim,
    The homely nurse doth all she can
To make her foster-child, her inmate Man,
    Forget the glories he hath known,
And that imperial palace whence he came.

Behold the Child among his new-born blisses,
A six years' darling of a pigmy size!
See, where 'mid work of his own hand he lies,
Fretted by sallies of his Mother's kisses,
With light upon him from his Father's eyes!
See, at his feet, some little plan or chart,

Some fragment from his dream of human life,
Shaped by himself with newly-learnèd art;
    A wedding or a festival,
    A mourning or a funeral,
      And this hath now his heart,
    And unto this he frames his song:
      Then will he fit his tongue
To dialogue of business, love, or strife;
    But it will not be long
    Ere this be thrown aside,
    And with new joy and pride
The little actor cons another part,
Filling from time to time his "humorous stage"
With all the Persons, down to palsied Age,
That Life brings with her in her equipage;
    As if his whole vocation
    Were endless imitation.

Thou, whose exterior semblance doth belie
    Thy soul's immensity;
Thou best philosopher, who yet dost keep
Thy heritage, thou eye among the blind,
That, deaf and silent, read'st the eternal deep,
Haunted for ever by the eternal mind, —
    Mighty Prophet! Seer blest!
    On whom those truths do rest,

Which we are toiling all our lives to find,
In darkness lost, the darkness of the grave;
Thou, over whom thy Immortality
Broods like the Day, a master o'er a slave,
A presence which is not to be put by;
     To whom the grave
Is but a lonely bed without the sense or sight
    Of day or the warm light,
A place of thought where we in waiting lie;
Thou little Child, yet glorious in the might
Of heaven-born freedom on thy being's height,
Why with such earnest pains dost thou provoke
The years to bring the inevitable yoke,
Thus blindly with thy blessedness at strife?
Full soon thy soul shall have her earthly freight,
And custom lie upon thee with a weight,
Heavy as frost, and deep almost as life!
    O joy! that in our embers
    Is something that doth live,
    That nature yet remembers
    What was so fugitive!
The thought of our past years in me doth breed
Perpetual benediction: not indeed
For that which is most worthy to be blest; —
Delight and liberty, the simple creed
Of childhood, whether busy or at rest,

With new-fledged hope still fluttering in his
      breast: —
      Not for these I raise
      The song of thanks and praise;
    But for those obstinate questionings
    Of sense and outward things,
    Fallings from us, vanishings;
    Blank misgivings of a Creature
Moving about in worlds not realized,
High instincts before which our mortal Nature
Did tremble like a guilty thing surprised:
      But for those first affections,
      Those shadowy recollections,
      Which, be they what they may,
Are yet the fountain light of all our day,
Are yet a master light of all our seeing;
Uphold us, cherish, and have power to make
Our noisy years seem moments in the being
Of the eternal Silence: truths that wake,
      To perish never:
Which neither listlessness, nor mad endeavour,
      Nor Man nor Boy,
Nor all that is at enmity with joy,
Can utterly abolish or destroy!
      Hence, in a season of calm weather,
        Though inland far we be,

Our souls have sight of that immortal sea
　　　Which brought us hither,
　　　Can in a moment travel thither,
　　And see the children sport upon the shore,
And hear the mighty waters rolling evermore.

Then sing, ye birds, sing, sing a joyous song!
　　　And let the young lambs bound
　　　As to the tabor's sound!
We in thought will join your throng,
　　Ye that pipe and ye that play,
　　Ye that through your hearts to-day
　　Feel the gladness of the May!
What though the radiance which was once so
　　bright
Be now for ever taken from my sight,
　　Though nothing can bring back the hour
Of splendour in the grass, of glory in the flower;
　　We will grieve not, rather find
　　Strength in what remains behind;
　　In the primal sympathy
　　Which having been must ever be;
　　In the soothing thoughts that spring
　　Out of human suffering,
　　In the faith that looks through death,
In years that bring the philosophic mind.

And O ye Fountains, Meadows, Hills, and Groves,
Think not of any severing of our loves!
Yet in my heart of hearts I feel your might;
I only have relinquish'd one delight
To live beneath your more habitual sway.
I love the brooks which down their channels fret;
Even more than when I tripp'd lightly as they;
The innocent brightness of a new-born Day
      Is lovely yet;
The clouds that gather round the setting sun
Do take a sober colouring from an eye
That hath kept watch o'er man's mortality;
Another race hath been, and other palms are won.
Thanks to the human heart by which we live,
Thanks to its tenderness, its joys, and fears,
To me the meanest flower that blows can give
Thoughts that do often lie too deep for tears.

               William Wordsworth.

Time, Real and Imaginary

An Allegory

ON the wide level of a mountain's head
(I knew not where, but 'twas some faery place),
Their pinions, ostrich-like, for sails outspread,
Two lovely children run an endless race,
      A sister and a brother!

This far outstripp'd the other;
Yet ever runs she with reverted face,
And looks and listens for the boy behind:
For he, alas! is blind!
O'er rough and smooth with even step he pass'd,
And knows not whether he be first or last.

Samuel Taylor Coleridge.

Part III
Childhood

A Child's Grace

HERE a little child I stand
Heaving up my either hand;
Cold as paddocks though they be,
Yet I lift them up to Thee,
For a benison to fall
On our meat and on us all. Amen.

Robert Herrick.

The Picture of Little T. C.
In a Prospect of Flowers

SEE with what simplicity
This nymph begins her golden days!
In the green grass she loves to lie,
And there with her fair aspect tames
The wilder flowers, and gives them names;
But only with the roses plays,
And them does tell
What colour best becomes them, and what smell.

Who can foretell for what high cause
This darling of the Gods was born?
Yet this is she whose chaster laws

The wanton Love shall one day fear,
And, under her command severe,
    See his bow broke and ensigns torn.
      Happy who can
Appease this virtuous enemy of man!

    O then let me in time compound
   And parley with those conquering eyes,
    Ere they have tried their force to wound;
Ere with their glancing wheels they drive
In triumph over hearts that strive,
    And them that yield but more despise:
      Let me be laid,
Where I may see the glories from some shade.

    Meantime, whilst every verdant thing
   Itself does at thy beauty charm,
    Reform the errors of the Spring;
Make that the tulips may have share
Of sweetness, seeing they are fair,
    And roses of their thorns disarm;
      But most procure
That violets may a longer age endure.

    But O, young beauty of the woods,
   Whom Nature courts with fruits and flowers,

Gather the flowers, but spare the buds;
Lest Flora, angry at thy crime
To kill her infants in their prime,
  Do quickly make th' example yours;
    And ere we see,
Nip in the blossom all our hopes and thee.

Andrew Marvell.

The Nymph and the Fawn

WITH sweetest milk and sugar first
I it at my own fingers nursed;
And as it grew, so every day
It waxed more white and sweet than they.
It had so sweet a breath! And oft
I blushed to see its foot more soft
And white, shall I say than my hand?
Nay, any lady's of the land.
  It is a wondrous thing how fleet
'T was on those little silver feet;
With what a pretty skipping grace
It oft would challenge me the race;
And, when't had left me far away,
'T would stay, and run again, and stay;
For it was nimbler much than hinds,
And trod as if on the four winds.

I have a garden of my own,
But so with roses overgrown,
And lilies, that you would it guess
To be a little wilderness;
And all the spring-time of the year
It only lovèd to be there.
Among the beds of lilies I
Have sought it oft, where it should lie,
Yet could not, till itself would rise,
Find it, although before mine eyes;
For, in the flaxen lilies' shade,
Is like a bank of lilies laid.
Upon the roses it would feed,
Until its lips e'en seem to bleed
And then to me 't would boldly trip,
And print those roses on my lip.
But all its chief delight was still
On roses thus itself to fill,
And its pure virgin limbs to fold
In whitest sheets of lilies cold:
Had it lived long, it would have been
Lilies without, roses within.

Andrew Marvell.

A Child

A CHILD's a plaything for an hour;
  Its pretty tricks we try
For that or for a longer space —
  Then tire, and lay it by.

But I knew one that to itself
  All seasons could control;
That would have mock'd the sense of pain
  Out of a grievèd soul.

Thou straggler into loving arms,
  Young climber-up of knees,
When I forget thy thousand ways
  Then life and all shall cease.

Mary Lamb.

Three Years She Grew

THREE years she grew in sun and shower;
Then Nature said, A lovelier flower
  On earth was never sown;
This Child I to myself will take;
She shall be mine, and I will make
  A lady of my own.

Myself will to my darling be
Both law and impulse: and with me

The girl, in rock and plain,
In earth and heaven, in glade and bower,
Shall feel an overseeing power
    To kindle and restrain.

She shall be sportive as the fawn
That wild with glee across the lawn
    Or up the mountain springs;
And hers shall be the breathing balm,
And hers the silence and the calm
    Of mute insensate things.

The floating clouds their state shall lend
To her; for her the willow bend;
    Nor shall she fail to see
Even in the motions of the storm
Grace that shall mould the maiden's form
    By silent sympathy.

The stars of midnight shall be dear
To her; and she shall lean her ear
    In many a secret place
Where rivulets dance their wayward round,
And beauty born of murmuring sound
    Shall pass into her face.

And vital feelings of delight
Shall rear her form to stately height,

Her virgin bosom swell;
Such thoughts to Lucy I will give
While she and I together live
　　Here in this happy dell.

　　Thus Nature spake — The work was **done** —
How soon my Lucy's race was run!
　　She died, and left to me
This heath, this calm and quiet scene;
The memory of what has been,
　　And never more will be.

William Wordsworth.

Mater Dolorosa

I'D a dream to-night
　　As I fell asleep,
O! the touching sight
　　Makes me still to weep:
Of my little lad,
　　Gone to leave me sad,
Aye, the child I had,
　　But was not to keep.

As in heaven high,
　　I my child did seek,
There, in train, came by
　　Children fair and meek,

Each in lily white,
  With a lamp alight;
Each was clear to sight,
  But they did not speak.

Then, a little sad,
  Came my child in turn,
But the lamp he had
  O! it did not burn!
He, to clear my doubt,
  Said, half turn'd about,
'Your tears put it out;
  Mother, never mourn.'

William Barnes.

Letty's Globe

WHEN Letty had scarce pass'd her third glad year,
And her young, artless words began to flow,
One day we gave the child a colour'd sphere
Of the wide earth, that she might mark and know,
By tint and outline, all its sea and land.
She patted all the world; old empires peep'd
Between her baby fingers; her soft hand
Was welcome at all frontiers. How she leap'd,
And laugh'd, and prattled in her world-wide bliss;

But when we turn'd her sweet unlearnéd eye
On our own isle, she raised a joyous cry,
'Oh, yes, I see it, Letty's home is there!'
And, while she hid all England with a kiss,
Bright over Europe fell her golden hair.

                              Charles Tennyson-Turner.

The Toys

MY little son, who look'd from thoughtful eyes,
And moved and spoke in quiet grown-up wise,
Having my law the seventh time disobey'd,
I struck him, and dismiss'd
With hard words and unkiss'd,
His mother, who was patient, being dead.
Then, fearing lest his grief should hinder sleep,
I visited his bed,
But found him slumbering deep,
With darken'd eyelids, and their lashes yet
From his late sobbing wet.
And I, with moan,
Kissing away his tears, left others of my own;
For, on a table drawn beside his head,
He had put, within his reach,
A box of counters and a red-vein'd stone,
A piece of glass abraded by the beach
And six or seven shells,

A bottle with bluebells,
And two French copper coins, ranged there with
      careful art,
To comfort his sad heart.

So when that night I pray'd
To God, I wept, and said:
Oh, when at last we lie with trancéd breath,
Not vexing Thee in death,
And Thou rememberest of what toys
We made our joys,
How weakly understood
Thy great commanded good, —
Then, fatherly not less
Than I whom Thou hast moulded from the clay,
Thou 'lt leave Thy wrath, and say,
'I will be sorry for their childishness.'

                      Coventry Patmore.

Mother to Babe

FLECK of sky you are,
Dropped through branches dark,
  O my little one, mine!
Promise of the star
Outpour of the lark;
  Beam and song divine.

See this precious gift,
Steeping in new birth
   All my being, for sign
Earth to Heaven can lift,
Heaven descend on earth,
   Both in one be mine!

Life in light you glass
When you peep and coo,
   You, my little one, mine!
Brooklet chirps to grass,
Daisy looks in dew
   Up to dear sunshine.

George Meredith.

Bed in Summer

In winter I get up at night
And dress by yellow candle-light.
In summer, quite the other way,
I have to go to bed by day.

I have to go to bed and see
The birds still hopping on the tree,
Or hear the grown-up people's feet
Still going past me in the street.

And does it not seem hard to you,
When all the sky is clear and blue,
And I should like so much to play,
To have to go to bed by day?

Robert Louis Stevenson.

My Bed is a Boat

My bed is like a little boat;
　Nurse helps me in when I embark;
She girds me in my sailor's coat
　And starts me in the dark.

At night, I go on board and say
　Good-night to all my friends on shore;
I shut my eyes and sail away
　And see and hear no more.

And sometimes things to bed I take,
　As prudent sailors have to do;
Perhaps a slice of wedding-cake,
　Perhaps a toy or two.

All night across the dark we steer;
　But when the day returns at last,
Safe in my room, beside the pier,
　I find my vessel fast.

Robert Louis Stevenson.

The Wind

I SAW you toss the kites on high
And blow the birds about the sky;
And all around I heard you pass,
Like ladies' skirts across the grass —
    O wind, a-blowing all day long,
    O wind, that sings so loud a song!

I saw the different things you did,
But always you yourself you hid.
I felt you push, I heard you call,
I could not see yourself at all —
    O wind, a-blowing all day long,
    O wind, that sings so loud a song!

O you that are so strong and cold,
O blower, are you young or old?
Are you a beast of field and tree,
Or just a stronger child than me?
    O wind, a-blowing all day long,
    O wind, that sings so loud a song!

Robert Louis Stevenson.

North-West Passage

I

Good Night

WHEN the bright lamp is carried in,
The sunless hours again begin;
O'er all without, in field and lane,
The haunted night returns again.

Now we behold the embers flee
About the firelit hearth; and see
Our faces painted as we pass,
Like pictures, on the window-glass.

Must we to bed indeed? Well then,
Let us arise and go like men,
And face with an undaunted tread
The long black passage up to bed.

Farewell, O brother, sister, sire!
O pleasant party round the fire!
The songs you sing, the tales you tell,
Till far to-morrow, fare ye well!

Robert Louis Stevenson

From the painting by W. B. Richmond

II

Shadow March

All round the house is the jet-black night;
  It stares through the window-pane;
It crawls in the corners, hiding from the light,
  And it moves with the moving flame.

Now my little heart goes a-beating like a drum,
  With the breath of the Bogie in my hair;
And all round the candle the crooked shadows come,
  And go marching along up the stair.

The shadow of the balusters, the shadow of the
    lamp,
  The shadow of the child that goes to bed —
All the wicked shadows coming tramp, tramp,
    tramp,
  With the black night overhead.

Robert Louis Stevenson.

"Adveniat Regnum Tuum"

Thy kingdom come! Yea, bid it come!
But when Thy kingdom first began
On earth, Thy kingdom was a home,
A child, a woman, and a man.

The child was in the midst thereof,
O, blessed Jesus, holiest One!
The centre and the fount of love,
Mary and Joseph's little Son.

Wherever on the earth shall be
A child, a woman, and a man,
Imaging that sweet trinity
Wherewith Thy kingdom first began,

Establish there Thy kingdom! Yea,
And o'er that trinity of love
Send down, as in Thy appointed day,
The brooding spirit of Thy Dove!

Katharine Tynan.

The Only Child

Lest he miss other children, lo!
His angel is his playfellow.
A riotous angel two years old,
With wings of rose and curls of gold.

There on the nursery floor together
They play when it is rainy weather,
Building brick castles with much pain,
Only to knock them down again.

Two golden heads together look
An hour long o'er a picture-book,
Or, tired of being good and still,
They play at horses with good will.

And when the boy laughs you shall hear
Another laughter silver-clear,
Sweeter than music of the skies,
Or harps, or birds of Paradise.

Two golden heads one pillow press,
Two rosebuds shut for heaviness.
The wings of one are round the other
Lest chill befall his tender brother.

All day, with forethought mild and grave,
The little angel's quick to save.
And still outruns with tender haste
The adventurous feet that go too fast.

From draughts, from fire, from cold and stings,
Wraps him within his gauzy wings;
And knows his father's pride, and shares
His happy mother's tears and prayers.

Katharine Tynan.

Part IV
Night

Mydnyght

MYDNYGHT was cum, and every vitall thing
With swete sound slepe theyr weary lyms did rest:
The beasts were still, the lytle byrdes that syng
Now sweetely slept besides theyr mothers brest,
The olde and all were shrowded in theyr nest.
The waters calme, the cruel seas did ceas,
The wuds, the fyeldes, and all things held theyr
    peace.

The golden stars wer whyrlde amyd theyr race,
And on the earth did laugh with twinkling light,
When eche thing nestled in his restyng place,
Forgat dayes payne with pleasure of the nyght:
The hare had not the greedy houndes in sight,
The fearful dear of death stood not in doubt,
The partrydge drempt not of the falcon's foot.

The ougly beare nowe myndeth not the stake,
Nor howe the cruell mastyves do him tear;
The stag lay still unroused from the brake,
The fomy boar feard not the hunter's spear.
All thing was still in desert, bush, and brear,
With quyet heart now from their travailes rest,
Soundly they slept in midst of all their nest.

    Thomas Sackville, Lord Buckhurst.

Hymn to Diana

QUEEN and Huntress, chaste and fair,
  Now the sun is laid to sleep,
Seated in thy silver chair,
    State in wonted manner keep:
      Hesperus entreats thy light,
      Goddess excellently bright.

Earth, let not thy envious shade
  Dare itself to interpose;
Cynthia's shining orb was made
    Heaven to clear when day did close.
      Bless us then with wished sight,
      Goddess excellently bright.

Lay thy bow of pearl apart
  And thy crystal shining quiver;
Give unto the flying hart
    Space to breathe, how short soever:
      Thou that makest day of night,
      Goddess excellently bright.

                                    Ben Jonson.

The Evening Knell

SHEPHERDS all, and Maidens fair,
Fold your flocks up, for the air
'Gins to thicken, and the sun
Already his great course hath run.
See the dew-drops how they kiss
Every little flower that is:
Hanging on their velvet heads,
Like a rope of crystal beads.
See the heavy clouds low falling,
And bright Hesperus down calling
The dead night from under ground,
At whose rising mists unsound,
Damps, and vapours fly apace,
Hovering o'er the wanton face
Of these pastures, where they come,
Striking dead both bud and bloom;
Therefore from such danger lock
Everyone his 'loved flock,
And let your dogs lie loose without,
Lest the wolf come as a scout
From the mountain, and e're day
Bear a lamb or kid away,
Or the crafty thievish fox,
Break upon your simple flocks:

To secure yourselves from these
Be not too secure in ease;
Let one eye his watches keep,
Whilst the other eye doth sleep;
So you shall good shepherds prove,
And forever hold the love
Of our great God. Sweetest slumbers
And soft silence fall in numbers
On your eye-lids: so farewell,
Thus I end my evening knell.

John Fletcher.

"Oft, on a Plat of Rising Ground"

Oft, on a plat of rising ground,
I hear the far-off Curfeu sound
Over some wide-water'd shore,
Swinging slow with sullen roar;
Or, if the air will not permit,
Some still removèd place will fit,
Where glowing embers through the room
Teach light to counterfeit a gloom;
Far from all resort of mirth,
Save the cricket on the hearth,
Or the bellman's drowsy charm
To bless the doors from nightly harm.

IOHN MILTON

DRAWN AND ETCHED MDCCLX BY I.B.CIPRIANI A TVSCAN FROM
A PICTVRE PAINTED BY CORNELIVS IOHNSON MDCXVIII NOW IN THE
POSSESSION OF THOMAS HOLLIS OF LINCOLN'S INNE F.R. AND A.S.S.

WHEN I WAS YET A CHILD NO CHILDISH PLAY
TO ME WAS PLEASING ALL MY MIND WAS SET
SERIOVS TO LEARN AND KNOW AND THENCE TO DO
WHAT MIGHT BE PVBLIC GOOD MY SELF I THOVGHT
BORN TO THAT END BORN TO PROMOTE ALL TRVTH
ALL RIGHTEOVS THINGS
                                    PARAD. REG.

John Milton

From the etching by G. B. Cipriani after
the painting by Cornelis Janssens

Or let my lamp at midnight hour
Be seen in some high lonely tower,
Where I may oft out-watch the Bear
With thrice-great Hermes, or unsphere
The spirit of Plato, to unfold
What worlds or what vast regions hold
The immortal mind, that hath forsook
Her mansion in this fleshly nook:
And of those demons that are found,
In fire, air, flood or under ground,
Whose power hath a true consent
With planet, or with element.

John Milton.

Evening on Calais Beach

It is a beauteous evening, calm and free;
The holy time is quiet as a Nun
Breathless with adoration; the broad sun
Is sinking down in its tranquillity;
The gentleness of heaven is on the sea:
Listen! the mighty Being is awake,
And doth with his eternal motion make
A sound like thunder — everlastingly.
Dear Child! dear Girl! that walkest with me here,
If thou appear untouch'd by solemn thought,

Thy nature is not therefore less divine:
Thou liest in Abraham's bosom all the year;
And worship'st at the Temple's inner shrine,
God being with thee when we know it not.
William Wordsworth.

Song to the Evening Star

STAR that bringest home the bee,
And sett'st the weary labourer free!
If any star shed peace, 't is Thou
   That send'st it from above,
Appearing when Heaven's breath and brow
   Are sweet as hers we love.

Come to the luxuriant skies,
Whilst the landscape's odours rise,
Whilst far-off lowing herds are heard
   And songs when toil is done,
From cottages whose smoke unstirr'd
   Curls yellow in the sun.

Star of love's soft interviews,
Parted lovers on thee muse;
Their remembrancer in Heaven
   Of thrilling vows thou art,
Too delicious to be riven
   By absence from the heart.
Thomas Campbell.

To the Night

SWIFTLY walk over the western wave,
    Spirit of Night!
Out of the misty eastern cave
Where, all the long and lone daylight,
Thou wovest dreams of joy and fear
Which make thee terrible and dear, —
    Swift be thy flight!

Wrap thy form in a mantle gray
    Star-inwrought;
Blind with thine hair the eyes of Day,
Kiss her until she be wearied out:
Then wander o'er city and sea and land,
Touching all with thine opiate wand —
    Come, long-sought!

When I arose and saw the dawn,
    I sigh'd for thee;
When light rode high, and the dew was gone,
And soon lay heavy on flower and tree,
And the weary Day turn'd to his rest
Lingering like an unloved guest,
    I sigh'd for thee.

Thy brother Death came, and cried
    Wouldst thou me?
Thy sweet child Sleep, the filmy-eyed,
Murmur'd like a noon-tide bee
Shall I nestle near thy side?
Wouldst thou me? — And I replied
    No, not thee!

Death will come when thou art dead,
    Soon, too soon —
Sleep will come when thou art fled;
Of neither would I ask the boon
I ask of thee, belovèd Night —
Swift be thine approaching flight,
    Come soon, soon!

                    Percy Bysshe Shelley.

To the Moon

ART thou pale for weariness
Of climbing heaven, and gazing on the earth,
    Wandering companionless
Among the stars that have a different birth, —
And ever-changing, like a joyless eye
That finds no object worth its constancy?

                    Percy Bysshe Shelley.

Sunset Wings

To-night this sunset spreads two golden wings
    Cleaving the western sky;
Winged too with wind it is, and winnowings
Of birds; as if the day's last hour in rings
    Of strenuous flight must die.

Sun-steeped in fire, the homeward pinions sway
    Above the dovecote-tops;
And clouds of starlings, ere they rest with day,
Sink, clamorous like mill-waters, at wild play,
    By turns in every copse:

Each tree heart-deep the wrangling rout re-
        ceives, —
    Save for the whirr within,
You could not tell the starlings from the leaves;
Then one great puff of wings, and the swarm
        heaves
    Away with all its din.

Even thus Hope's hours, in ever-eddying flight,
    To many a refuge tend;
With the first light she laughed, and the last light
Glows round her still; who natheless in the night
    At length must make an end.

And now the mustering rooks innumerable
 Together sail and soar,
While for the day's death, like a tolling knell,
Unto the heart they seem to cry, Farewell,
 No more, farewell, no more!

Is Hope not plumed, as 't were a fiery dart?
And oh! thou dying day,
Even as thou goest must she too depart,
And Sorrow fold such pinions on the heart
 As will not fly away?

Dante Gabriel Rossetti.

Part V
Sleep

Sleep

By him lay heavy Sleep, the cousin of Death,
Flat on the ground, and still as any stone,
A very corpse, save yielding forth a breath:
Small keep took he, whom Fortune frownèd on,
Or whom she lifted up into the throne
    Of high renown; but, as a living death,
    So, dead alive, of life he drew the breath.

The body's vest, the quiet of the heart,
The travail's ease, the still night's fear was he,
And of our life in earth the better part:
Reaver of sight, and yet in whom we see
Things oft that tide, and oft that never be:
    Without respect, esteeming equally
    King Croesus' pomp, and Irus' poverty.
                Thomas Sackville, Lord Buckhurst.

"With How Sad Steps, O Moon"

With how sad steps, O Moon, thou climb'st the
    skies!
How silently, and with how wan a face!
What, may it be that even in heav'nly place
That busy archer his sharp arrows tries!
Sure, if that long-with-love-acquainted eyes
Can judge of love, thou feel'st a lover's case,

I read it in thy looks; thy languish'd grace,
To me, that feel the like, thy state descries.
Then, e'en of fellowship, O Moon, tell me,
Is constant love deem'd there but want of wit?
Are beauties there as proud as here they be?
Do they above love to be loved, and yet
Those lovers scorn whom that love doth possess?
Do they call virtue, there, ungratefulness?

Sir Philip Sidney.

"Come, Sleep! O Sleep"

COME, Sleep! O Sleep, the certain knot of peace,
The baiting-place of wit, the balm of woe,
The poor man's wealth, the prisoner's release,
Th' indifferent judge between the high and low;
With shield of proof shield me from out the press
Of those fierce darts Despair at me doth throw:
O make in me these civil wars to cease;
I will good tribute pay, if thou do so.
Take thou of me smooth pillows, sweetest bed,
A chamber deaf to noise and blind to light,
A rosy garland and a weary head:
And if these things, as being thine by right,
Move not thy heavy grace, thou shalt in me,
Livelier than elsewhere, Stella's image see.

Sir Philip Sidney.

Sir Philip Sidney

From the engraving by George Vertue
after the painting by Isaac Oliver

Care-Charmer Sleep

CARE-Charmer Sleep, son of the sable night,
Brother to Death, in silent darkness born:
Relieve my languish and restore the light;
With dark forgetting of my care, return,
And let the day be time enough to mourn
The shipwrack of my ill-adventured youth:
Let waking eyes suffice to wail their scorn
Without the torment of the night's untruth.
Cease dreams, the images of day desires,
To model forth the passions of the morrow;
Never let rising sun approve you liars,
To add more grief to aggravate my sorrow.
Still let me sleep, embracing clouds in vain,
And never wake to feel the day's disdain.

Samuel Daniel.

The Cypress Curtain

THE cypress curtain of the night is spread,
And over all a silent dew is cast.
The weaker cares, by sleep are conquered:
But I alone, with hideous grief aghast,
In spite of Morpheus' charms, a watch do keep
Over mine eyes, to banish careless sleep.

Yet oft my trembling eyes through faintness
    close,
And then the Map of Hell before me stands;
Which ghosts do see, and I am one of those
Ordained to pine in sorrow's endless bands,
Since from my wretched soul all hopes are reft
And now no cause of life to me is left.

Grief, seize my soul! for that will still endure
When my crazed body is consumed and gone;
Bear it to thy black den! there keep it sure
Where thou ten thousand souls dost tire upon!
Yet all do not afford such food to thee
As this poor one, the worser part of me.

                        Thomas Campion.

Come, Sleep

Come, Sleep, and with thy sweet deceiving,
    Lock me in delight awhile;
      Let some pleasing dreams beguile
      All my fancies; that from thence
      I may feel an influence,
    All my powers of care bereaving!

Though but a shadow, but a sliding,
    Let me know some little joy!

We that suffer long annoy
Are contented with a thought,
Through an idle fancy wrought:
Oh, let my joys have some abiding!

John Fletcher.

Invocation to Sleep

CARE-charming Sleep, thou easer of all woes,
Brother to Death, sweetly thyself dispose
On this afflicted prince; fall like a cloud
In gentle showers; give nothing that is loud
Or painful to his slumbers; easy, light,
And as a purling stream, thou son of Night
Pass by his troubled senses; sing his pain
Like hollow murmuring wind or silver rain;
Into this prince gently, O gently, slide,
And kiss him into slumbers like a bride.

John Fletcher.

Dawn

FLY hence, shadows, that do keep
Watchful sorrows charmed in sleep!
Tho' the eyes be overtaken,
Yet the heart doth ever waken
Thoughts chained up in busy snares
Of continual woes and cares:

Love and griefs are so exprest
As they rather sigh than rest.
Fly hence, shadows, that do keep
Watchful sorrows charmed in sleep!

John Ford.

On a Quiet Conscience

CLOSE thine eyes, and sleep secure;
Thy soul is safe, thy body sure.
He that guards thee, he that keeps,
Never slumbers, never sleeps.
A quiet conscience in the breast
Has only peace, has only rest.
The wisest and the mirth of kings
Are out of tune unless she sings:
Then close thine eyes in peace and sleep
    secure,
No sleep so sweet as thine, no rest so sure.

King Charles I.

An Anodyne

As in the night I restless lie
I the watch-candle keep in eye;
The innocent I often blame,
For the slow wasting of its flame.

John Fletcher

From the engraving by George Vertue

Sweet ease! O whither are you fled!
With one short slumber ease my head!

My curtain oft I draw away,
Eager to see the morning ray;
But when the morning gilds the skies,
The morning no relief supplies.
To me, alas! the morning light
Is as afflictive as the night.

My vigorous cries to God ascend,
O! will not God my cries attend?
Can God paternal love forbear,
Can God reject a filial prayer?
Is there in Heaven for me no cure,
Why do I then such pains endure?

My flesh in torture oft repines
At what God for my good designs;
My spirit the repiner chides,
Submissive to God's will abides:
God my disease and temper weighs,
No pang superfluous on me lays.

Why should I then my pains decline,
Inflicted by pure love divine?

Let them run out their destined course,
And spend upon me all their force:
Short pains can never grievous be,
Which work a blest eternity.

Thomas Ken.

To Sleep

A FLOCK of sheep that leisurely pass by
One after one; the sound of rain, and bees
Murmuring; the fall of rivers, winds and seas,
Smooth fields, white sheets of water, and pure
      sky;
By turns have all been thought of, yet I lie
Sleepless; and soon the small birds' melodies
Must hear, first utter'd from my orchard trees,
And the first cuckoo's melancholy cry.
Even thus last night, and two nights more I lay,
And could not win thee, Sleep! by any stealth:
So do not let me wear to-night away:
Without Thee what is all the morning's wealth?
Come, blessèd barrier between day and day,
Dear mother of fresh thoughts and joyous health!

William Wordsworth.

To Sleep

O soft embalmer of the still midnight!
    Shutting with careful fingers and benign
Our gloom-pleased eyes, embower'd from the
    light,
    Enshaded in forgetfulness divine;
O soothest Sleep! if so it please thee, close,
    In midst of this thine hymn, my willing eyes,
Or wait the amen, ere thy poppy throws
    Around my bed its lulling charities;
    Then save me, or the passèd day will shine
Upon my pillow, breeding many woes;
Save me from curious conscience, that still lords
    Its strength for darkness, burrowing like a
    mole;
Turn the key deftly in the oilèd wards,
    And seal the hushèd casket of my soul.
John Keats.

The Magic Sleep

Year after year, unto her feet,
    She lying on her couch alone,
Across the purple coverlet
    The maiden's jet-black hair has grown,

On either side her trancèd form
  Forth streaming from a braid of pearl;
The slumbrous light is rich and warm,
  And moves not on the rounded curl.

The silk star-broider'd coverlid
  Unto her limbs itself doth mould,
Languidly ever; and, amid
  Her full black ringlets downward roll'd,
Glows forth each softly shadow'd arm
  With bracelets of the diamond bright:
Her constant beauty doth inform
  Stillness with love, and day with light.

She sleeps: her breathings are not heard
  In palace chambers far apart.
The fragrant tresses are not stirr'd,
  That lie upon her charmèd heart.
She sleeps: on either hand upswells
  The gold-fringed pillow lightly press'd:
She sleeps, nor dreams, but ever dwells
  A perfect form in perfect rest.

Alfred, Lord Tennyson.

Part VI
Charms

"You Spotted Snakes with Double Tongue"

You spotted snakes with double tongue,
    Thorny hedge-hogs be not seen;
Newts and blind-worms, do no wrong;
    Come not near our fairy-queen:
        Philomel, with melody,
        Sing in our sweet lullaby;
Lulla, lulla, lullaby; lulla, lulla, lullaby;
        Never harm,
        Nor spell, nor charm,
        Come our lovely lady nigh;
        So, good night, with lullaby.

Weaving spiders, come not here:
    Hence, you long-legged spinners, hence!
Beetles black, approach not near;
    Worm, nor snail, do no offence.
        Philomel, with melody,
        Sing in our sweet lullaby;
Lulla, lulla, lullaby; lulla, lulla, lullaby;
        Never harm,
        Nor spell, nor charm,
        Come our lovely lady nigh;
        So, good night, with lullaby.

William Shakespeare.

The Charm

Son of Erebus and Night,
Hie away; and aim thy flight,
Where consort none other fowl
Than the bat and sullen owl;
Where upon thy limber grass
Poppy and mandragoras
With like simples not a few
Hang for ever drops of dew.
Where flows Lethe without coil
Softly like a stream of oil.
Hie thee thither, gentle Sleep:
With this Greek no longer keep.
Thrice I charge thee by my wand,
Thrice with moly from my hand
Do I touch Ulysses' eyes,
And with the jaspis: then arise
Sagest Greek . . .

William Browne.

"Now the Hungry Lion Roars"

Now the hungry lion roars,
　And the wolf behowls the moon;
Whilst the heavy ploughman snores,
　All with weary task fordone.

Now the wasted brands do glow,
   Whilst the scritch-owl, scritching loud,
Puts the wretch that lies in woe
   In remembrance of a shroud.
Now it is the time of night
   That the graves, all gaping wide,
Everyone lets forth his sprite,
   In the churchway paths to glide:
And we fairies, that do run
   By the triple Hecate's team,
From the presence of the sun,
   Following darkness like a dream,
Now are frolic; not a mouse
Shall disturb this hallowed house:
I am sent with broom before,
To sweep the dust behind the door.

William Shakespeare.

The Charm

1st Witch. Thrice the brindled cat hath mewed.
2nd Witch. Thrice;   and   once   the   hedge-pig
              whined.
3rd Witch. Harpier cries: 'T is time, 't is time.
1st Witch. Round about the cauldron go:
             In the poison'd entrails throw.

Toad, that under coldest stone
Days and nights has thirty-one
Sweltered venom sleeping got,
Boil thou first i' th' charmèd pot!

All.   Double, double toil and trouble;
Fire, burn; and cauldron, bubble.

2nd Witch. Fillet of a fenny snake,
In the cauldron boil and bake;
Eye of newt and toe of frog,
Wool of bat and tongue of dog,
Adder's fork and blind-worm's sting,
Lizard's leg and owlet's wing,
For a charm of powerful trouble,
Like a hell-broth boil and bubble.

All.   Double, double toil and trouble;
Fire, burn; and cauldron bubble.

3rd Witch. Scale of dragon, tooth of wolf;
Witches' mummy; maw and gulf
Of the ravined salt-sea shark,
Root of hemlock, digg'd i' th' dark,
Liver of blaspheming Jew,
Gall of goat, and slips of yew,
Slivered in the moon's eclipse,
Nose of Turk, and Tartar's lips,
Finger of birth-strangled babe,

William Shakespeare
From the engraving by Martin Droeshout

     Ditch-delivered by a drab,
     Make the grue thick and slab;
     Add thereto a tiger's chaudron,
     For the ingredients of our cauldron.
All.   Double, double toil and trouble;
     Fire, burn; and cauldron, bubble.
2nd Witch. Cool it with a baboon's blood,
     Then the charm is firm and good.
         William Shakespeare.

Dream-Pedlary

If there were dreams to sell,
  What would you buy?
Some cost a passing bell;
  Some a light sigh,
That shakes from Life's fresh crown
Only a rose-leaf down.
If there were dreams to sell,
Merry and sad to tell,
And the crier rang the bell,
  What would you buy?

A cottage lone and still,
  With bowers nigh,
Shadowy, my woes to still,
  Until I die.

Such peace from Life's fresh crown
Fain would I shake me down.
Were dreams to have at will,
This would best heal my ill,
   This would I buy.

      Thomas Lovell Beddoes.

The Owl

WHEN cats run home and light is come,
  And dew is cold upon the ground,
And the far-off stream is dumb,
  And the whirring sail goes round,
  And the whirring sail goes round;
    Alone and warming his five wits,
    The white owl in the belfry sits.

When merry milkmaids click the latch,
  And rarely smells the new-mown hay,
And the cock hath sung beneath the thatch
  Twice or thrice his roundelay,
  Twice or thrice his roundelay;
    Alone and warming his five wits,
    The white owl in the belfry sits.

      Alfred, Lord Tennyson.

The Fairies

Up the airy mountain,
    Down the rushy glen,
We dare n't go a-hunting
    For fear of little men;
Wee folk, good folk,
    Trooping all together;
Green jacket, red cap,
    And white owl's feather!

Down along the rocky shore
    Some make their home,
They live on crispy pancakes
    Of yellow tide-foam;
Some in the reeds
    Of the black mountain lake,
With frogs for their watch-dogs,
    All night awake.

High on the hill-top
    The old King sits;
He is now so old and grey
    He 's nigh lost his wits.
With a bridge of white mist
    Columbkill he crosses,
On his stately journeys
    From Slieveleague to Rosses;

Or going up with music
    On cold, starry nights,
To sup with the Queen
    Of the gay Northern Lights.

They stole little Bridget
    For seven years long;
When she came down again,
    Her friends were all gone.
They took her lightly back,
    Between the night and morrow,
They thought that she was fast asleep,
    But she was dead with sorrow.
They have kept her ever since
    Deep within the lake,
On a bed of flag-leaves,
    Watching till she wake.

By the craggy hill-side,
    Through the mosses bare,
They have planted thorn-trees
    For pleasure here and there.
Is any man so daring
    As dig one up in spite,
He shall find the thornies set
    In his bed at night.

Up the airy mountain,
 Down the rushy glen,
We dare n't go a-hunting
 For fear of little men;
Wee folk, good folk,
 Trooping all together;
Green jacket, red cap,
 And white owl's feather.
     William Allingham.

Robin Goodfellow

FROM Oberon, in Fairy-land,
The King of ghosts and shadows there,
Mad Robin I, at his command,
Am sent to view the night-sports here.
  What revel rout
  Is kept about,
 In every corner where I go,
  I will o'ersee,
  And merry be,
 And make good sport with ho, ho, ho!

More swift than lightning can I fly
About this airy welken soon,
And, in a minute's space descry
Each thing that's done below the moon.

There's not a hag
Or ghost shall wag,
Or cry 'ware goblins! where I go;
But, Robin, I
Their feats will spy,
And send them home with ho, ho, ho!

Whene'er such wanderers I meet,
As from their night-sports they trudge home,
With counterfeiting voice I greet,
And call them on with me to roam,
Through woods, through lakes,
Through bogs, through brakes,
Or else, unseen, with them I go,
All in the nick
To play some trick,
And frolic it, with ho, ho, ho!

Sometimes I meet them like a man,
Sometimes an ox, sometimes a hound,
And to a horse I turn me can,
To trip and trot about them round.
But if to ride,
My back they stride,
More swift than wind away I go,
O'er hedge and lands,
Through pools and ponds,
I hurry, laughing, ho, ho, ho!

By wells and rills, in meadows green,
We nightly dance in heyday guise;
And to our fairy king and queen
We chant our moonlight minstrelsies.
        When larks 'gin sing
        Away we fling;
    And babes new-born steal as we go,
        And elf in bed
        We leave instead,
    And wend us laughing, ho, ho, ho!

From hag-bred Merlin's time have I
Thus nightly revell'd to and fro;
And for my pranks men call me by
The name of Robin Good-fellow.
        Fiends, ghosts and sprites,
        Who haunt the nights,
    The hags and goblins do me know;
        And beldames old
        My feats have told
    So valé, valé! ho, ho, ho!

Anonymous.

Part VII

Dirges

Tuwhoo, Tuwhit, Tuwhit, Tuwhoo-o-o

SWEET Suffolk owl, so trimly dight
With feathers like a lady bright,
Thou sing'st alone, sitting by night,
  Te whit, te whoo!
Thy note, that forth so freely rolls,
With shrill command the mouse controls,
And sings a dirge for dying souls,
  Te whit, te whoo!

Thomas Vauter.

"Why Art Thou Slow,
Thou Rest of Trouble, Death"

WHY art thou slow, thou rest of trouble, Death,
  To stop a wretch's breath,
That calls on thee, and offers her sad heart
  A prey unto thy dart?
I am not young nor fair; be, therefore, bold:
  Sorrow hath made me old,
Deformed and wrinkled; all that I can crave
  Is quiet in my grave.
Such as live happy, hold long life a jewel;
  But to me thou art cruel,

If thou end not my tedious misery
　　　　And I soon cease to be.
Strike, and strike home, then; pity unto me,
In one short hour's delay, is tyranny.

Philip Massinger.

A Dirge

CALL for the robin-redbreast and the wren,
Since o'er shady graves they hover,
And with leaves and flowers do cover
The friendless bodies of unburied men.
Call unto his funeral dole
The ant, the field-mouse, and the mole,
To rear him hillocks that shall keep him warm,
And (when gay tombs are robbed) sustain no
　　　　harm;
But keep the wolf far thence, that 's foe to men,
For with his nails he 'll dig them up again.

John Webster.

Dirge

HARK, now everything is still,
The screech-owl and the whistler shrill,
Call upon our dame aloud,
And bid her quickly don her shroud!

Much you had of land and rent;
Your length in clay's now competent:
A long war disturbed your mind;
Here your perfect peace is signed.
Of what is 't fools make such vain keeping?
Sin their conception, their birth weeping,
Their life a general mist of error,
Their death a hideous storm of terror.
Strew your hair with powders sweet,
Don clean linen, bathe your feet,
And — the foul fiend more to check —
A crucifix let bless your neck:
'T is now full tide 'tween night and day;
End your groan, and come away.

John Webster.

Upon a Child That Died

HERE a pretty baby lies
Sung asleep with lullabies:
Pray be silent and not stir
Th' easy earth that covers her.

Robert Herrick.

Indexes

Index to Authors
With First Lines of their Poems

The Table

Or Index to First Lines

𝔉𝔦𝔫𝔦𝔰